THE
Horse Breeds
POSTER BOOK

Lisa H. Hiley

Photographs by Bob Langrish

Are you one of those kids who'd rather think, read, and talk about horses than just about anything else? Lots of people feel that way about these beautiful animals. Even though horses are strong and powerful, they can also be kind and gentle.

For hundreds of years, people and horses have had a special relationship. Before motors and engines, horses helped us in many ways. They worked alongside farmers in the fields, pulled settlers traveling to the West, hauled delivery wagons in cities, and carried doctors to their patients. Nowadays, even though we don't need them to do all those things, there are still millions of horses in North America.

Some kids are lucky enough to have horses of their very own to care for and ride. If you don't have your own horse, you might take lessons at a nearby stable or have friends who let you visit their horses. But you don't have to be near real, live horses to love them and want to learn all about them. And the more you know when you do get to be around horses, the better off you'll be.

This book will surround you with wonderful horses of all kinds. Here are thirty posters for you to hang on your wall, with information about each breed on the back. Whether you're just beginning to learn about horses or you already know a lot about them, you'll love these pictures, and you'll probably find out something new.

Happy Trails!

Icelandic
Horse

Icelandic Horse

• • • • • • • •

Though small (12.3 to 13.2 hands), Icelandic Horses are sturdy, with strong legs and big heads. Their thick coats and shaggy manes and tails protect them in the harshest weather. These horses can carry heavy loads on rocky, steep terrain. In addition to the walk, trot, and canter or gallop, they have the **tolt** (a smooth, running walk that is very comfortable for the rider). Many also perform the **skeid,** a very fast gait in which the feet on the same side of the body move together. These little horses are intelligent and gentle, have remarkable stamina, and are very hardy. Icelandic Horses come in a rainbow of colors, including paint, but chestnuts and bays are seen most frequently.

What They're Good At

In Iceland, these horses are used in a variety of competitions, as well as for trail riding and rounding up the many sheep that live there. In other countries, they have become very popular as pleasure horses.

Where They Come From

The Icelandic Horse has been bred for centuries in Iceland, where it is the only breed of horse.

Did You Know?

This is one of the purest breeds in the world. There has been no crossing with other breeds for more than 1,000 years.

Belgian
Draft Horse

Belgian Draft Horse

· · · · · · · ·

These big, strong horses have short legs compared to their bodies, large heads, and powerful hindquarters. They have some **feathering** (a fringe of hair) on their legs and feet, but not a lot. Belgians used to come in several colors, but today the breed is known for its bright **chestnut** or **sorrel** color: golden red with a flaxen mane and tail. A white stripe on the nose and four white socks are prized markings but are not always present. Belgians are at least 16 hands tall and can be as tall as 18 hands.

What They're Good At

Belgians are often seen competing in pulling contests at fairs, where they are capable of pulling loads of more than 3,000 pounds. They also make good carriage horses and are sometimes driven as a team of four.

Where They Come From

As their name suggests, these horses come from Belgium, where farmers bred strong horses to pull their plows.

Did You Know?

Many centuries ago, the Belgian was used to carry knights in heavy armor into battle.

Welsh Pony

• • • • • • • •

There are two kinds of Welsh ponies: the sturdy **cob** (or small horse) and the more refined riding pony. Both have lovely heads that show the influence of Arabian ancestry in the dished face and dainty muzzle. They have short backs, strong legs, and rounded hindquarters. They come in all solid colors but are most often gray. White markings are found, but not pinto coloring. Welsh ponies can range from under 12 to over 13.2 hands high.

What They're Good At

Welsh ponies can do nearly anything asked of them. They are good athletes and are used in harness and under saddle in every kind of event. They are famous for their natural jumping ability, even temperament, and ground-covering trot.

Where They Come From

As their name suggests, Welsh ponies originated in Wales, where for many centuries they lived in semi-wild herds and were used by farmers to carry heavy loads.

Did You Know?

Welsh ponies pulled chariots in the time of the ancient Romans.

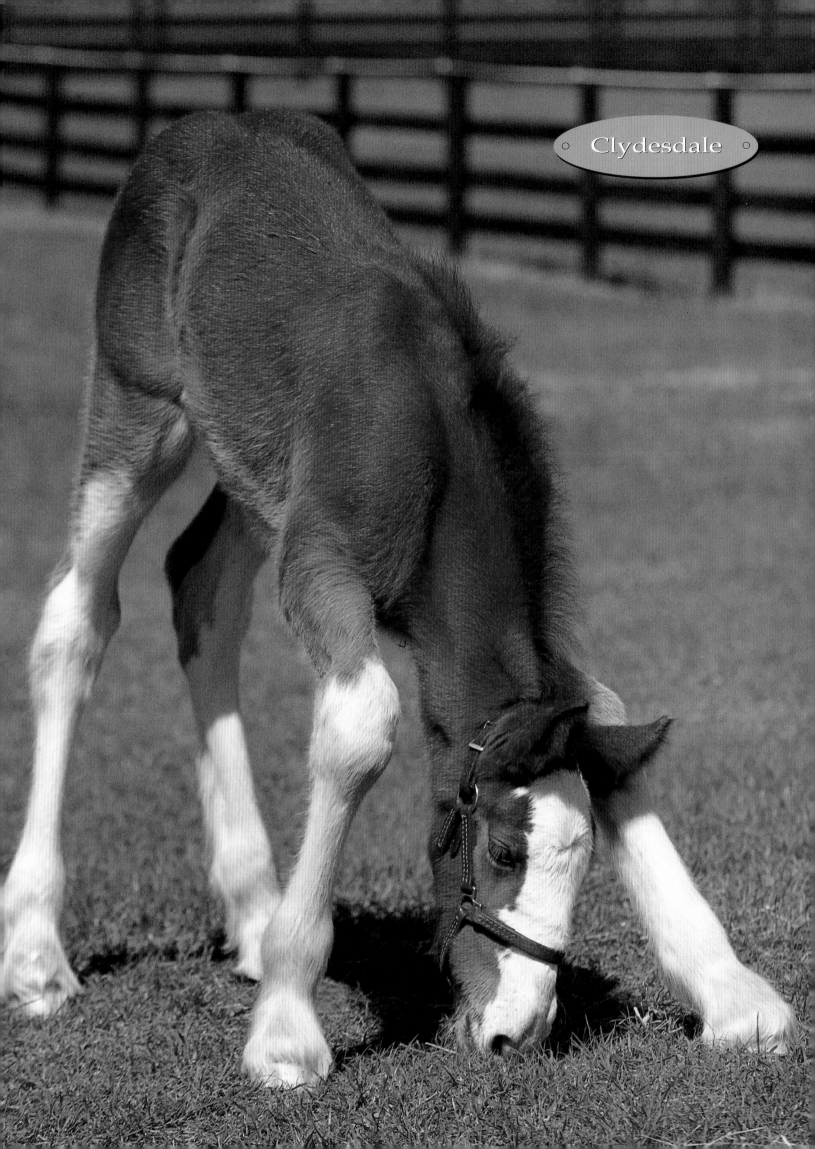

Clydesdale

Clydesdale

· · · · · · · ·

While not as sturdily built as many other draft breeds, Clydesdales are large, strong horses with powerful necks. Their legs are long and straight, with big, round hooves and long feathers that swish when they move. The breed is known for its light, springy action at the trot. They can be 16 to 18 hands tall and are usually dark brown or bay. Roans are also seen. White blazes and stockings are common.

What They're Good At

The handsome Clydesdale is a popular horse for heavy hitches and is often seen in teams of six, eight, and even ten at once.

Where They Come From

Clydesdales come from an area of Scotland near the river Clyde. They were first used by farmers but became popular for pulling heavy delivery wagons in cities.

Did You Know?

Teams of Clydesdales participate in parades at many amusement parks and other attractions. They are perhaps most famous as the mascots of a certain brand of beer.

Shetland Pony

Shetland Pony

• • • • • • • •

Shetland ponies stand no more than 42 inches at the withers. They have thick coats and long, heavy manes and tails. Their faces are somewhat dished, with small ears and large, expressive eyes. All colors are found except Appaloosa-type spots. Black and brown are the most common. Shetlands are friendly, curious, and intelligent, but they don't hesitate to take advantage of a lazy or unkind rider. In the United States, a taller, slimmer type of Shetland has been developed for the show ring. This type is often more high spirited and less docile than its plump, furry cousin.

What They're Good At

Long ago, Shetlands pulled plows, carried heavy loads to market, and worked in coal mines. Today, Shetlands are beloved as children's ponies and family pets. They make excellent harness ponies as well. It is not unusual to see them in circuses.

Where They Come From

A very old breed, the Shetland pony has lived for centuries on the Shetland and Orkney Islands north of Scotland, but little is known about how they came there in the first place.

Did You Know?

Pound for pound, Shetlands are said to be the strongest horses of all. They can pull twice their own weight!

Tennessee
Walking Horse

Tennessee Walking Horse

● ● ● ● ● ● ●

Long and lean, Walkers, as they are called, have refined heads and arched necks. All colors, including pinto, are permitted, and 15.2 hands is the average height (they range from 14.3 to 17 hands). Walkers are known for their pleasant personalities and intelligence. They can canter, but rather than trotting, they naturally fall into a gait called the **running walk,** a speedy version of the regular walk that is very comfortable for the rider. The horse can keep up the running walk for a long time without tiring.

What They're Good At

Though primarily a saddle horse, the Walker is also shown in harness. Most people value it for trail riding, and it is used in both English and Western pleasure events.

Where They Come From

Walkers were bred in the rocky hills and valleys of Tennessee by plantation owners who spent many hours each day in the saddle. They have Morgan, Thoroughbred, Standardbred, and American Saddlebred blood.

Did You Know?

At the running walk, the Walker's hind foot steps past the front foot by as much as 18 inches. At each step, it nods its head as though it is keeping time. Some Walkers clack their teeth as they nod along.

Connemara
Pony

Connemara Pony

• • • • • • • •

Wonderful ponies for young riders, Connemaras are tough, hardy, and "easy keepers," meaning that they can live well on plain food and rough shelter. Their sturdy bodies and short legs give them a rectangular shape. They are usually gray or brown, though other colors, such as dun, are also seen. Paint coloring is not allowed. Connemaras are among the tallest of the pony breeds, standing up to 15 hands, though 14.2 is average. These ponies are known for their stamina, good nature, and pleasant personalities.

What They're Good At

Although they are good at lots of things, Connemaras excel at jumping. They make good dressage mounts as well.

Where They Come From

Bred in the Connemara region of western Ireland, these rugged ponies were used by farmers to haul loads of rocks out of their fields and haul loads of fertilizer into the fields. They pulled a plow all week and pulled the family to church on Sundays.

Did You Know?

Every August, hundreds of Connemara Ponies travel to Clifden, Connemara, Ireland, for the world's largest Connemara show.

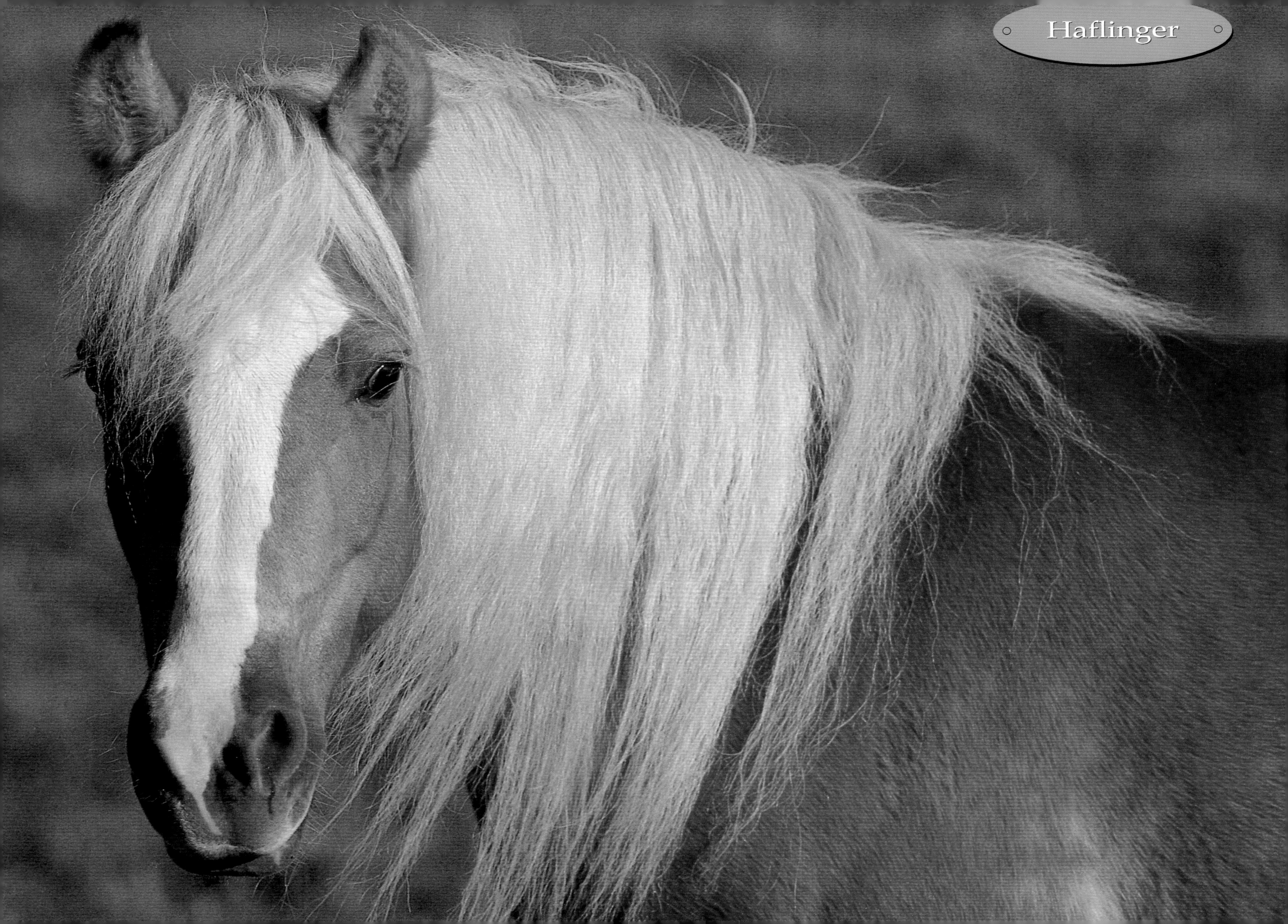
Haflinger

Haflinger

●●●●●●●●

With their round muscles and short necks, these sturdy horses look like miniature draft horses. They stand 13.2 to 14.3 hands high and can be any shade of chestnut, from reddish gold to light chocolate. Their thick, full manes and tails are much lighter, ranging from **flaxen** (pale gold) to white. Haflingers have strong legs and good feet that rarely give trouble. They love people and are prized for their intelligence, willingness to learn, and eagerness to please.

What They're Good At

Bred in steep mountain terrain, Haflingers are sure-footed and have a short, quick stride. They are often seen in harness but are excellent riding horses in many disciplines. They make good **vaulting** (gymnastic) horses and are used in therapeutic riding programs for the disabled.

Where They Come From

The Haflinger was developed in the late 1800s in the Tyrolean mountain region of what is now Austria and northern Italy. A half-Arabian stallion crossed with a native mountain pony resulted in the modern bloodline.

Did You Know?

Haflingers grow slowly and are not usually fully trained until they are four years old. However, they also live a long time and can still work into their forties.

Andalusian

• • • • • • • •

(an-da-<u>loo</u>-zhun)

Andalusians carry their beautiful heads on long, arched necks. Their manes and tails are silky and thick, with a heavy forelock often covering the eyes. With long, muscular bodies set on strong, straight legs, Andalusians move with great style and grace. They are very intelligent, have kind **dispositions** (personalities), and can be high spirited. Most Andalusians are some shade of gray. The rest (about 20 percent) are either bay or black. They stand between 15 and 16.2 hands high.

What They're Good At

While still not a very common horse in the United States, the Andalusian is becoming known for its many talents. It is a wonderful dressage horse and a valued circus performer. A beautiful carriage horse, it can also jump well.

Where They Come From

This horse comes from the province of Andalusia in Spain. Drawings of horses that look very much like today's Andalusians have been found in primitive cave paintings.

Did You Know?

The Andalusian, an ancient breed, was the favorite horse of European kings and queens during the Middle Ages.

Chincoteague Pony

· · · · · · · ·

(<u>chink</u>-oh-teeg)

Chincoteague ponies don't all look alike, but they tend to have pretty faces and compact bodies. They are 12 to 13 hands high and come in all colors; pinto is common. The ponies are friendly and curious around people. Although thought of as wild, they are actually under the care of the Chincoteague Volunteer Fire Company, which rounds them up twice a year for veterinary care.

What They're Good At

Once tamed, Chincoteague ponies make excellent children's mounts and are used all over the United States in many kinds of competitions and pleasure riding.

Where They Come From

Chincoteague Ponies live on the island of Assateague, off the coast of Virginia and Maryland. One legend tells of the wreck of a Spanish ship carrying a cargo of horses to the New World. When the ship broke up, the horses swam to shore and have lived there ever since.

Did You Know?

Chincoteague ponies were made famous with the true story of *Misty*, written by Marguerite Henry. When a storm destroyed much of the island's grass in 1962, children from all over the United States sent their allowances to help buy food for the ponies.

American Saddlebred

• • • • • • • •

These tall horses (16 to 17 hands) carry their heads and tails high. Their long, flowing manes and tails need a lot of care for the show ring. They are spirited horses that enjoy showing off in the ring, but they are friendly and willing to work hard. Usually bay, chestnut, black, or brown, Saddlebreds often have splashy white markings on their legs and face.

What They're Good At

Commonly called the "peacock of the show ring," Saddlebreds are also used as trail horses, jumpers, and driving horses. Some Saddlebreds perform at the walk, trot, and canter. Others can also do the **slow gait** and the **rack**, in which the horse lifts its feet very high and looks as though it is dancing.

Where They Come From

The flashy Saddlebred was developed in the American South in the 1800s by crossing Thoroughbreds with an old breed called the Narragansett Pacer, which no longer exists as a separate breed.

Did You Know?

Sometimes Saddlebreds wear false tails in the show ring to fill out their own. Their manes are left long and flowing, often with one braid displaying a colorful ribbon.

Rocky Mountain Horse

• • • • • • • •

This rare breed is popular in Kentucky and southern Ohio, where people prize its smooth gait and calm temperament. A medium-sized horse (14.2 to 16 hands), the Rocky Mountain Horse has a natural **amble** or smooth, fast walk that is very comfortable for the rider and enables the horse to go for miles without tiring. These horses come in all solid colors — never pinto or Appaloosa or with any white above the knee. They are known for their calm and steady natures.

What They're Good At

Rocky Mountain Horses are ridden for pleasure and are good endurance competitors. They can pull a carriage or plow but are not naturally gifted jumpers.

Where They Come From

This breed originated in Kentucky in the early 1900s and is well suited to the rugged terrain and tough living of the mountains. In 1986, an association was formed to preserve the Rocky Mountain Horse and develop breed standards.

Did You Know?

A common color for Rocky Mountain Horses is dark chocolate with a cream or silver mane and tail — a very unusual color combination for a horse.

Bashkir
Curly

Bashkir Curly

• • • • • • • •

These horses are noted for their hair, which can be slightly wavy or tightly curled. Their manes and tails are crinkly, too. In the summer, they shed their heavy coats and might look smooth. They even shed their manes and sometimes their tails for the summer! They are usually of medium size and are sturdy and surefooted. Curlies are very smart, gentle, and loving.

What They're Good At

Though still quite rare in the United States, the Curly has performed well in nearly any horse event you can imagine. It makes an outstanding trail and endurance horse and, with its love of people, is a favorite with children.

Where They Come From

The origin of the Curly horse in this country is a mystery. Records show that the Sioux Indians had curly-coated horses in the early 1800s. What is known for sure is that a father and son found three curly horses on their ranch in the mountains of Nevada and began breeding them. The American Bashkir Curly Registry was set up in 1971 to protect the breed.

Did You Know?

Many people who are allergic to other horses are able to ride Curlies because of their hypoallergenic coats.

Selle Français

• • • • • • • • •

(sell fron-<u>seh</u>)

The conformation of these horses can vary quite a bit because of the many breeds in their background. However, Selle Français horses tend to be tall (15.3 to 17 hands), with long bodies and necks. Their attractive heads have long ears, and their profiles can be either straight or slightly dished. They can be any color, but are usually chestnut. They are known for their springy, extended movement at all gaits, and their knee action is quite high for a riding horse.

What They're Good At

Naturally athletic, the Selle Français is an outstanding jumper and is often seen in international competition. It is also used in racing (against breeds other than Thoroughbreds), endurance riding, and dressage.

Where They Come From

These horses were developed in France by crossing native horses with Thoroughbreds.

Did You Know?

A Selle Français horse can have as a **sire** (father) a Thoroughbred, an Anglo-Arab, or a French Trotter and still be registered as a Selle Français.

Peruvian
Paso

Peruvian Paso

• • • • • • • •

(peh-<u>roo</u>-veey-un <u>pah</u>-so)

These muscular riding horses have curved necks with long, flowing manes. They are of medium size (14.1 to 15.2 hands), with strong, round backs. Their ears turn in at the tips. They can be any solid color, without a lot of white marking. These horses have a natural tendency to move their shoulders in a circular pattern rather than straight back and forth like most horses do. They were bred for three distinct gaits (the flat walk, the *paso llano,* and the *sobreandando*), which they display from birth. Even at top speed, Peruvian Pasos maintain their very smooth, comfortable movement.

What They're Good At

Because of their comfortable gaits, Pasos are wonderful trail horses, used on ranches in their native land and becoming increasingly popular in the United States. They are also shown at all gaits by riders in native costume.

Where They Come From

The Peruvian Paso was developed in Peru more than four centuries ago from horses brought to the New World by the Spanish. A similar breed, the Paso Fino, was developed in Central and South America and the Caribbean.

Did You Know?

Peruvian Pasos are always shown without horseshoes.

Pony of the Americas

Pony of the Americas

· · · · · · · ·

The Pony of the Americas (POA) looks like a miniature Appaloosa (11.5 to 14 hands). It has Appaloosa coloring, including mottled skin around the muzzle and eyes and striped hooves. Balanced and well muscled, POAs have fine heads with slightly **dished** (curved-in) faces. They have clean, strong legs and powerful shoulders and hindquarters. Developed as children's mounts, they are known for their gentle dispositions and nice manners.

What They're Good At

A good all-around horse for young riders, the POA is a favorite pleasure mount, a willing competitor, and a smart cow pony. It is also shown in halter classes and in harness.

Where They Come From

A relatively new breed, the first POA resulted from the accidental crossing of a Shetland pony with an Appaloosa. Today, the bloodline includes the Welsh pony, the Arabian, and the Quarter Horse as well.

Did You Know?

The first POA was called Black Hand because of the pattern of spots on his flank.

Miniature
Horse

Miniature Horse

• • • • • • • •

(Falabella Miniature Horse)

The first Miniature Horses (or minis, as most people call them) looked like dwarfs, with heavy heads and stumpy legs. Careful breeding has produced an animal that looks like a proper horse, only smaller, standing 34 inches or less. Miniatures tend to have very full, thick manes and tails. Because they have been bred to be companions, most minis are curious and friendly, and enjoy being around people. Like ponies, they can be mischievous and playful.

What They're Good At

They are wonderful companions, both for people and for other horses. While not suitable for riding, even by children, minis can pull an adult in a small cart, and are often driven in teams. They can sometimes be seen in **liberty** horse acts (with no saddle or bridle) at the circus.

Where They Come From

These tiny horses were first bred in the 1860s by the Falabella family of Argentina, using feral horses descended from Spanish breeds.

Did You Know?

While the height of most horses is measured at the withers, minis are measured at the last hair of the mane.

Morgan

Morgan

·······

There are two types of Morgans. The "classic" type has round muscles, sturdy legs, and a strong neck. The "show" type is more slender and holds its neck and tail up high. Both have slightly **dished** (curved-in) faces with small ears and kind faces. Morgans are known for being calm, friendly, and sensible. They stand between 14.2 and 15.2 hands high and are nearly always bay, dark brown, or chestnut. Palomino coloring is also allowed.

What They're Good At

Morgans are very versatile, which means they can do almost anything. People use them for trail riding, driving, farmwork, showing, even herding cows. They are popular as police horses and were used by the military for many years.

Where They Come From

All of today's Morgan horses can be traced back to one stallion, a sturdy little workhorse named Figure. He belonged to a singing teacher named Justin Morgan in Vermont more than two hundred years ago. He could pull heavy loads or plow a field all day and then have enough energy to run races and win them.

Did You Know?

Morgans live a long time. Figure was thirty-two when he died, and many Morgans live into their thirties if they have good care.

Gypsy Vanner Horse

• • • • • • • •

Gypsy Vanners are small draft horses with an elegant look. They are a mix of Shire, Clydesdale, Friesian, and Dales Pony. Lush feathers on their lower legs swish when they move, and they have thick, heavy manes and tails. They have short, arched necks and short backs with rounded haunches. Although they can be any color, they are prized for spectacular **piebald** (black and white) or **skewbald** (brown and white) markings. Gypsy Vanner Horses were bred particularly to be kind, gentle, and intelligent.

What They're Good At

Developed to pull heavy caravans, these athletic horses have also proved to be good riding horses. They have great stamina and are easy to train.

Where They Come From

They were developed by Gypsies to pull their colorful caravans as they traveled about Great Britain. An American couple fell in love with their exotic looks and gentle natures, and they imported four horses to the United States in the late 1990s.

Did You Know?

There are only a few dozen Gypsy Vanners in the United States, and the breed itself has been developed only during the past sixty years or so.

Percheron

Percheron

· · · · · · · ·

(purr-chur-on)

These large draft horses show some Arab ancestry in their elegant heads and small hooves. They are well rounded, with heavy shoulders and haunches and short, thick necks. They have a little feathering on their legs but not as much as some other draft horses. Ranging in height from 15.2 to 17.2 hands, Percherons can be any shade of gray or black. They are gentle, steady horses.

What They're Good At

Long used as a warhorse, the Percheron became a popular plow and cart horse, capable of pulling heavy loads. Today Percherons are used as carriage horses both singly and in teams. They are shown in halter classes, in harness, and even under saddle.

Where They Come From

These horses were first bred in the Perche district of France to carry knights into battle.

Did You Know?

The Percheron's wide, flat back makes it a popular horse for bareback circus riders and vaulters. In the circus, they are sometimes called "rosinbacks," because of the sticky powder sprinkled on them to help acrobatic riders keep their balance while standing up.

Glossary

Bay A number of shades of brown, from mahogany to auburn (reddish), with black mane and tail and often black on the legs as well.

Blaze A white marking down the center of the face. A narrow blaze is a **stripe;** a horse with a blaze covering the eyes is called **bald-faced.**

Buckskin Tan or yellow coloring with black mane and tail; often with a dark stripe down the back and stripes on the legs.

Chestnut Deep reddish brown coloring with mane and tail the same color or lighter.

Cutting A Western competition in which horse and rider separate a steer from the rest of the herd and keep it from turning back to join the others.

Dished face A concave profile in which the face curves in slightly below the eyes rather than being completely straight.

Draft horse A large, heavily muscled horse bred for pulling heavy loads, plowing, logging, and other hard work.

Dressage A combination of precise movements that display a high level of training on the part of both horse and rider.

Endurance riding A competition that tests the ability of horse and rider to cover long distances over often rough ground without becoming exhausted.

Feathering A fringe of hair around the lower legs, often found in draft horse breeds.

Gray A mixture of black and white hairs that can be any shade from almost white to nearly black. Pure white or black horses are unusual.

Hand The standard measurement of height. A hand is 4 inches. The number of hands is measured from the top of the withers.

Liberty horses Horses that perform "at liberty," without rider or restraint; often seen in circuses.

Palomino A color that can range from pale gold to bright copper with a **flaxen** (almost white) mane and tail.

Penning A Western event in which a team of three riders drives out three cows from a large herd and pens them in a separate enclosure.

Pinto Patches of white on a brown or black coat (or vice versa); mane and tail can be solid or a mixture of two colors.

Pleasure horse A horse of any breed that is comfortable to ride, well mannered, and attractive.

Pony A small horse measuring 14.2 hands (58 inches) at the withers.

Registered horse A horse of any breed that is eligible to join the official breed registry because of its parentage. For some breeds, having one registered parent is enough.

Roan A mixture of dark and light hairs, giving the coat a mottled or speckled appearance. "Blue roan" mixes black and white hairs; "red or strawberry roan" mixes brown or red and white hairs.

Roman nose A convex profile, in which the nose bulges out somewhat below the eyes rather than being completely straight.

Roping A variety of Western competition designed to show the rider's skill in roping cattle while riding, usually at a gallop.

Socks Color above the ankle but below the knee.

Sorrel A Western term for light chestnut (red) coloring — often with lighter mane and tail.

Stockings White or black coloring on the legs that goes above the knee.

Withers The top of a horse's shoulders, where the neck meets the body. Some horses have high, bony withers, while others have flat or round ones.

The mission of Storey Publishing is to serve our customers
by publishing practical information that encourages
personal independence in harmony with the environment.

Edited by Deborah Burns
Art direction by Meredith Maker
Photo consultant: Maddie J. Delaney
Design and production by Eugenie S. Delaney
Photographs © Bob Langrish

10 9 8 7 6 5

Printed in China by Elegance
Library of Congress Cataloging-in-Publication Data
Hiley, Lisa.
    The horse breeds poster book / By Lisa Hiley.
        p. cm.
Contents: American saddlebred — American standardbred — Andalusian — Appaloosa — Arabian — Bashkir curly — Belgian —
Chincoteague — Clydesdale — Connemara pony — Friesian — Gypsy Vanner — Haflinger — Icelandic — Lipizzaner — Miniature
horse — Morgan — Mustang — Paint — Percheron — Pony of the Americas — Peruvian Pasa — Quarter horse — Rocky mountain
horse — Selle Français — Shetland pony— Tennessee walking horse — Thoroughbred — Trakehner — Welsh pony.
    ISBN-13: 978-1-58017-507-4 (alk. paper); ISBN-10: 1-58017-507-4 (alk. paper)
1. Horse breeds—Juvenile literature. 2. Horses—Juvenile literature.
    [1. Horse breeds. 2. Horses.] I. Title.
SF291.H55 2003
636.1'0022'2—dc21
                                                                                                                        2003004554